# Index

## A few complimentary life transformation Hacks with the art of driving!

**Pic.** Source-unsplash

# INDIAN ROADS

## YOUR GUIDE TO SAFE DRIVES

### The Comprehensive Handbook for On-Road Safe Drives in India

**SATISH SURESH KULKARNI**

Copyright © Satish Suresh Kulkarni 2024
All Rights Reserved.

ISBN 979-8-89519-511-6

This book has been published with all efforts taken to make the material error-free after the consent of the author. However, the author and the publisher do not assume and hereby disclaim any liability to any party for any loss, damage, or disruption caused by errors or omissions, whether such errors or omissions result from negligence, accident, or any other cause.

While every effort has been made to avoid any mistake or omission, this publication is being sold on the condition and understanding that neither the author nor the publishers or printers would be liable in any manner to any person by reason of any mistake or omission in this publication or for any action taken or omitted to be taken or advice rendered or accepted on the basis of this work. For any defect in printing or binding the publishers will be liable only to replace the defective copy by another copy of this work then available.

# Introduction

During the past 25 years of my professional journey into a new car as well as tire development and allied functions such as advanced driving, team training, safety, testing infrastructure and facilities developments, Pan-India as well as international collaborations for projects purposes, one thing I particularly observed that, nowadays -even though the most of the people who drives a car or owns a car, are not really aware of basic necessities or prerequisites of on-road drives. The recent data on transportation I studied during my doctoral program is quite disturbing, mainly looking at the data on casualties on Indian roads. Of course, in India, road infrastructure, as well as technology related to on-road travel, has also been developing rapidly in the last 10 years. However, lack of awareness about the prerequisites of on-road drives is still a big challenge in saving lives, experiencing uninterrupted peaceful journeys, and enjoying the incredible diversity of this great nation. Even during some of my lectures on on-road safety in renowned social clubs, I found that people who have owned multiple cars for years do not have some basic information on safety that can help them save lives. Hence, it is a must for every person doing on-road drives, whether for business, personal, explorations, site scenes or even for fun, to know basic prerequisites and some very useful tips that can help in saving not only the self-life of the driver but also co-passengers and other road users. One more important aspect of this unawareness is that every causality or unwanted on-road event also incurs huge costs in terms of property, infrastructure, health care, and business, which affect individuals as well as the public economy.

The purpose of this manual is to offer important tips, rules and very basic technical know-how for safe and enjoyable driving, travel experience particularly in India's various seasons, which include the monsoon that creates multiple challenges and varying traffic, road infrastructure and other road travel related situations that may come as surprise many times.

It goes over how to prepare for driving with the most essential tips about your car, defensive driving strategies, strategies to avoid various unexpected probable events and monsoon-like climate, road travel specific emergency response protocols. Since the rest of the climate is safer than the monsoon, readers can follow the appropriate advice and make judgments based on all the information in the book.

Last but not least, this book provides you with a life transformation hack with the Art of Driving.

- *Every tip in this book is aimed to equip you for your own safety, and uninterrupted road drives, hence please don't overlook any, even though you are driving car from long time outside India. Even though you are driving from long time in India, some exclusive tips and strategies given here are purely based on long professional experience which are rarely taught or informed in routine driver trainings or on-road travel guidelines.*

# About Author

**Satish S Kulkarni** contributes to this handbook with his 25 years of real-world experience in the automotive and tire industries. He has devoted his professional life to evaluating cars, related product improvements, and test facilities, always prioritizing the safety and comfort of car users both during and after product development. With a keen interest in Vehicle Dynamics, Satish has worked with top national and international specialists and conducted extensive testing on some of the best test track facilities globally. His extensive experience in thoroughly analyzing cars during and after development in various climatic and geographical situations in India and around the world highlights his in-depth knowledge of the industry.

Beyond his technical abilities, Satish has been instrumental in team developments, especially developments of advanced skills in driving, assessments of cars and related facilities as well as infrastructure. He has also played a significant role in organizational and road safety campaigns. Passionate about humanity, social impact, and his spiritual journey with the Heartfulness Organization (HFN), Satish aims to contribute more and more to the betterment of society and the nation. His vast experience and knowledge have solidly established him as a leading authority on driving skills, evaluating driver behavior, vehicles, and on-road safety awareness initiatives. He is consistently upgrading his skills in human transformation and believes that the art of driving can not only improve on-road experiences but can also transform the behavior and lives of drivers -if the right techniques and habits are adopted.

His upcoming book aims to share these life-transforming aspects of the Art of Driving in depth. Satish is also the founder of "The Transformation Driver," an upcoming planned NGO focusing on social and personal transformations, road safety awareness, and skill development. He believes that in India, the interplay between "driving behavior, traffic challenges, and ongoing developments in technology as well as infrastructure" is also a key contributor to businesses and the economy of the nation. His doctoral study highlights the details with probable solutions on this topic.

**This first book of Satish is an invaluable resource for anyone driving a car in India, whether professionally or just for fun. The goal of this book is to help and educate all those drivers driving cars in any terrain or climate in India or Asia. Readers can better prepare themselves, anticipate situations, improve their driving experience, and take hassle-free road journeys while also potentially saving lives by heeding the advice provided.**

**With the help of the practical tips in this guide, you'll be able to enjoy road excursions inexhaustibly and drive with more assurance, accountability, and safety. Some of which are purely outcome of Satish's vast experience, and they are rarely available for public to learn.**

# Acknowledgments

I am deeply grateful to all the individuals and mentors who have supported me in advancing my skills and capabilities in driving, vehicle dynamics evaluation, safety and technology. I am grateful to my friend Milind Patil who triggered my journey of driving with giving me the first driving lesson on a ground at my native place Kolhapur in 1993.I was not aware that this skill is going to be a major part of my career journey and area of passion.

I am grateful to all my friends, seniors in my nature lover, social, political and bureaucrat circle- who always supported me about my profession and passion. Your guidance, compliments and encouragement have been invaluable in my journey.

Special thanks to my colleagues, seniors, drivers, technicians and friends in the automotive and tire industry for your unwavering support and sharing your knowledge and expertise in last 25 years.

I also extend my heartfelt gratitude to my spiritual masters, brothers, and sisters in Heartfulness meditation. Your teachings, blessings, and guidance have profoundly transformed my inner condition and outlook on caring for people and the mother nature around me. Your influence has inspired me to integrate these values into my professional and personal life.

I am also grateful to all the cars, facilities, and resources that have supported my amazing professional journey.

Last but not least, I am grateful to my family: my mother, who educated me in automotive engineering through a lot of hardship; my brothers, who are always there; my wife Mrudula, kids Harshwardhan and Madhura who always trusted me about my driving even though all 4 of us experienced a major road event in 2016 escaping without a scratch and that too in a car not having any advance safety systems including ABS. Your trust, during all the repeating high-risk vehicle testing and evaluations as an integral part of my profession, is a real blessing in my life that encouraged me to observe, study, and evaluate at a deeper level.

**To all of you, Thank You for being part of my journey!**

**Appreciation and gratitude to all those who are trying to make roads safer in their best capacities in India!**

# Module 1

# Pre-Driving Preparations

The key to guaranteeing a secure and pleasurable driving experience on Indian roads starts far before you turn on your car. Making the necessary preparations before driving is essential for comfort, safety, and following traffic laws.

**This is a comprehensive 'How to' on getting ready before driving:**

Make sure you are Physically fit enough to drive and that you are not impaired by any medications. Verify that you have had enough sleep and are not tired. Steer clear of the wheel when you're anxious or stressed. Examine the car for any obvious damage. Verify the fluid levels in the engine, coolant, brakes, and windscreen washer. Make sure every seat belt is functioning properly. Store reflective triangles in your car so you may utilize them in the event of an emergency.

**Documents:** Driver's license is up-to-date. Registration Certificate. A copy of the insurance coverage and PUC certificate is up-to-date.

**General preparation:** For the best comfort, make sure the heating or cooling system is functional. Make sure everyone is buckled up in their seat belts during the drive. Kids need to be in age-appropriate chairs. Maintain your cell phone, which is charged and handy for emergency situations. If required, use hands-free technology. To minimize distractions, set up your entertainment system or music before you go for a drive. Have a list of contacts for emergencies close at hand.

By carefully adhering to the pre-driving procedures/basic checks prescribed in this book, you can improve road safety for both you and others. Always keep in mind that the first stages to a safe and happy driving experience in India are a well-prepared driver and a well-maintained car.

## 1.1 Vehicle Health /Roadworthiness and Preparation

**Even if you think your car is in good running condition; please consider following pre-checks:**

### 1.1.1 INSTRUMENT CLUSTER SYMBOLS (Vehicle Health Display):

– Refer vehicle owner manual to understand various warning & indicative symbols. This section will help you understand it ON THE GO to ensure all is well before you start your drive.

– Cluster symbols will be ON when you press/Switch ON the ignition first time & will goes Off as you start the engine (or motor in case of EV)

– Ensure no unwanted warning symbol (Battery, Engine check lamp, Oil lamp, Temperature, airbag, Doors, seat belt, TPMS-tire pressure) is ON after the vehicle is started.

– If any such symbol is ON after engine starts, it indicates that particular system is having an issue, please check, if needed get it checked and cleared by a professional.

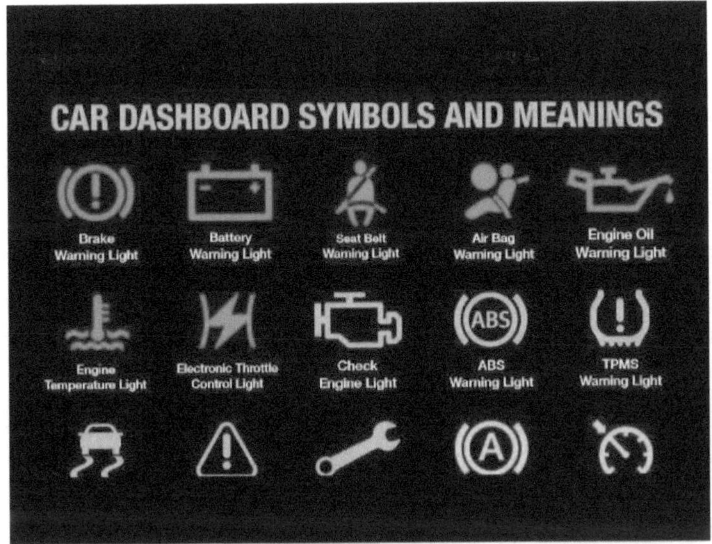


Source: gomechnic.in

## 1.1.2  TIREs: What to look for in it?

**Whatever input a driver gives to the car, finally it reaches to the tires for moving the car, hence tires are the most important component for your comfort and safety.**

— Inspect Tires: To **prevent hydroplaning, skidding** make sure the tires have a minimum of 2-3 mm of tread depth. Check any rubbed patch at tread with less than 2mm depth.

— verify the **wheel balancing and alignment** of the wheels. Check for any vibration or unwanted pull or drift that might cause the vehicle to drift from the straight path without the driver's input.

— Swap out as per OEM /Expert recommendation or replace deteriorated tires.

— Ensure that good tires among the set are placed at the drive axle (means good tyres at the front  if the car is front wheel drive car & vise versa)

— **Remember to ensure all 4 tires are of the same brand and tread pattern design.**

— Use Nitrogen or air to inflate tires. However, I will recommend air based on its ease of availability in most of the areas in INDIA.

**Remember: Using nitrogen also requires regular checks for inflation pressure, such as air.**

- *Tire to Road CONTACT AREA:* **It is just the size of your palm, but it is what keeps you safe; hence, never ignore the tire tread condition and Tire Pressure that makes this contact.**
- **Your tire side wall can pinch and cut beyond repair in the potholes or bump on a curb if you run it under-inflated, and the tire can burst in hot weather if it is over-inflated.**

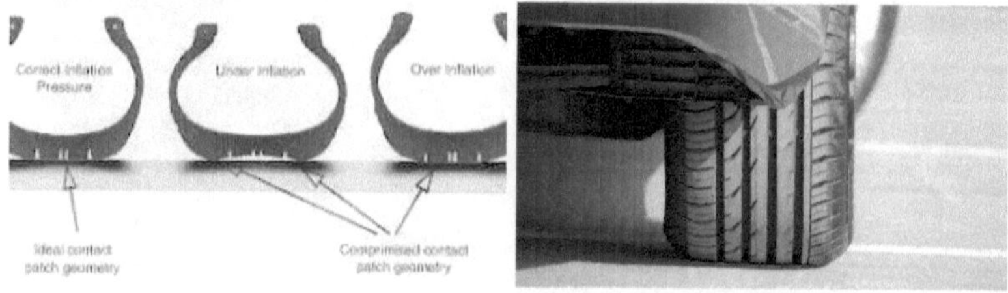


Fig. Tyre Road Contact Area (contact patch)

### 1.1.3 BRAKEs: Am I safe?

- Understanding the braking safety features of your car, ABS/ESC/AEB etc. is important.
- Verify the effectiveness of the brakes by driving straight & braking gradually. Make sure they are alert and not fatigued or spongy in feel.
- Make sure they are not over-responsive too, which may create risk during bumper-to-bumper traffic situations & on highways.

### 1.1.4 WIPERS and WINDSHIELD WASHER: What I must know?

Make sure your wipers are in good working order and that your washer fluid (which is combined with soapy water or shampoo to clean oil from windscreen glass) is topped up.

**When not to use wipers?** -If you feel someone has purposefully thrown something like an egg onto your windshield glass. Don't start wipers to clean it; the egg will spread on windshield glass and block the front view, and this will force you to stop. please try to sense the probable trouble.

**What should I Do?** - Don't stop the car, first reach at nearest safe/public place then clean the glass.

## 1.1.5 LIGHTINGS:

- **It not only shows you the way but also helps you to communicate with other road users.**

**Verify:** Headlights, taillights, side- indicators, and fog lights are operating properly, and glasses are dust-free

## 1.1.6 BATTERY: The Power bank of your car

- To prevent malfunctions, make sure the battery is in good condition.
- Check the electrolyte level and the state of charge (SOC) with a professional or use a hydrometer (you can get details on google about how to use it).

- **Make one last walk-around inspection of your car to make sure nothing has been missed. Before you set out on your journey, start the engine and let it idle for a short while to make sure everything is working well.**

## 1.2 Electric Vehicles

- Check the battery state of charge and ensure 100 % charge for long drives.
- Check for portable charger availability in the car.
- Check routes in advance for charging supports on the way.
- You can check with hotels on the way also for charging support on request.
- Check all the seals, ports& sockets are in proper condition and are debris-free
- Check with your car dealer that all softwares are up to date. Sometimes, software glitches create strange, unexpected issues in vehicles.
- If you are planning for a long trip in remote areas where charging stations are not available or where electricity supply is a probable issue, you may carry a portable generator set.

- On highways be more alert about other EVs around -as major collision of 2 EVs can be far more dangerous than IC engine cars.

## 1.3 Automatic Drive Assist (ADAS) Vehicle Checks and Cautions

- **What is ADAS?**

- Imagine having an invisible co-pilot in your car who is helping you Drive safely using smart technology. ADAS is like this co-pilot.

- **What does ADAS do?**

– Warns you in situations like too close with another car, someone in your blind spot, etc
– Help you park your car
– Help you in staying in your lane
– Automatically brakes if your car is about to collide with some object in front

- **Caution: The ADAS system works on a set algorithm of events and needs infrastructure support also to work, and in INDIA, there may be many unexpected events, road conditions, and under development infrastructures beyond design considerations. Hence, never drive fully dependent on ADAS features.**
- Check vehicle ADAS features. Get familiar with the functions from a car dealer or a known expert.
- While driving, try to assess which obstacles on the road ADAS cannot identify or respond to.
- Check and set AEB (auto emergency brake) for sensitivity level if provided by the manufacturer. If you do not feel confident or skeptical about rear vehicles while using AEB, **switch off the AEB function** -especially in high-traffic situations where vehicles are tailgating your car behind.
- **Check & get familiar with the LKA (Lane Keep Assist) function,**

**Remember, this function works only when roads are marked properly on both sides of the lane.**

## 1.4 Emergency Kit

– Keep an emergency kit on you that contains a flashlight, first aid box, basic tools, an umbrella, and a tow rope.
– For *High altitude places* like Leh, Ladakh: pl. Add an oxygen cylinder kit
– Always have a cell phone charger and portable inverter kit in your vehicle.

## 1.5  Plan and Verify Your Route in Advance

– Check for traffic updates and potentially flooded regions using navigation applications.

– Examine the various terrains of your trip, such as highways, hills, rough portions of road, cities and urban regions, forests, etc.

– Use an alternative route if needed but with the best possible cross-checking.

– Tell someone where you're going, check about routes, and when you expect to arrive.

– Please **don't just rely on GPS** routes. Verify to the best possible level, sometimes, GPS suggests some unwanted/unsafe shortcuts.

## Module 2

# Know this Before You Start Your Drive

- Make sure everything is firmly in place and doesn't interfere with your ability to see or move
- Adjust mirrors to get a proper side and rear view
- Adjust your Steering wheel Position so that you are comfortable to hold it for longer times
- Adjust your seat backrest angle and position such that you are taking proper control of the steering & pedals without any stress or extra efforts
- Wrong Steering wheel hold can lead you to misjudge the maneuvers
- Wrong seating posture can create extra fatigue on long drives and also health issues such as shoulder pains, backache, etc
- **Ideal steering hold style:**

Try to use **a 3'o clock -9 o'clock** or **2 o'clock -10 o'clock** hand position to hold the steering for better and balanced steering control. This position helps you better judge left and right sides in a balanced way when changing the directional course of the car or changing lanes.

- **You may feel a positive change in your other daily routine actions and responses -if you make this style a habit, Try this….**

# Module 3

# Defensive Driving Techniques: Especially for the Rainy Season

Rainy season driving in India is more difficult because of poor visibility, slick roads, underdeveloped roads, and sometimes unimaginable, erratic traffic patterns. This section offers defensive driving strategies designed to help you drive safely while it's raining a lot. On rainy roads, worn tires can drastically diminish traction. Rain frequently brings chilly weather, which can stress a poor cell; thus, having a strong battery is crucial. Go at a slower speed than normal. Gradually alter your direction and pace. Skidding can be brought on by abrupt brakes or abrupt bends. To increase visibility and make yourself more visible to other drivers. Avoid applying forceful brakes. Try to steer clear of big puddles when driving. They may create hydroplaning and conceal potholes. If you can't avoid it, proceed cautiously and gently. Use low beams or fog lights when it's raining heavily. Steer clear of high beams as they impede visibility due to reflections from fog. Roads covered in mud, oil, or leaves should be treated with additional caution because they become more slick when wet. Use indicators to communicate your goals well in advance. This aids other motorists in anticipating what you will do. In severe weather, pedestrians and bikers might not be as apparent, so pay attention to them.

Before you leave, check the road conditions and weather predictions. During the rainy season, traveling safely necessitates thorough planning and cautious driving. You may greatly lower the risks that come with rainy weather and make driving safer for both you and other people by adhering to these recommendations.

- Pay close attention to the Five Defensive Driving keys mentioned in the next section.
- **Defensive Driving Key 1. Speed Management**
- ***Remember, only driving slower does not guarantee your safety***
- ***Slow driving inappropriately can also lead to accidents***

- Keep in mind the following when driving at a high speed:

  a. The vehicle's road-holding grip and feedback you get from the steering might tell you this.
  b. You are maintaining safe ground space for handling emergencies in the surrounding area.
  c. Drive at a steady pace and give pedal inputs smoothly to improve vehicle control.

- Avoid abrupt acceleration, deceleration, and quick turns unless absolutely required.

- **Defensive Driving Key 2. Safe Distance**

- Reduced tire grip on the road causes stopping distance to rise if the road is even slightly wet.

- ***Remember, your antilock braking system feature (ABS) is a driver's assistance with stopping distance limitations, not a guarantee of safety in 100% of events. Use it with awareness.***

- Increase the following distance in heavy weather to account for decreased vision and longer braking distances.
- Maintain a safe distance from the vehicle ahead to allow enough stopping time.
- Maintaining distance also gives more time to respond during unexpected events with front vehicles or other road users.

- Be aware/alert of other road users' movements in car surroundings. Avoid staring at strangers.

- **Defensive Driving Key 3. Braking, Acceleration, and Overtaking:**

- Apply brakes gradually to prevent skidding.
- Use the soft tapping approach on the brakes to reduce speed gradually. This will help to keep the vehicle stable and comfortable for the occupants and prevent panic for the vehicle in the back.
- Gradually increase speed to avoid tire slipping

- **Overtaking:** Always *check for min. 2 vehicles ahead* (vehicle ahead and further objects/vehicles ahead of it -if any) in the row and side lane of your car when overtaking, This will give you more safer judgment of following other car and overtaking as well as lane changing.

- Be gentle. Always use side indicator headlights for communicating with other road users about your lane change and overtaking

- **Defensive Driving Key 4. Visibility**
- *Trust your eyes first (what you can see) rather than* relying only on your judgment.

  - If rain/fog is high, Use headlights even during the day to maximize visibility. - Stop aside with caution, especially if there are other cars passing by.
  - Use a demister switch, if needed, to avoid poor visibility due to mist on the front glass

**The Potato Hack**: If you forget to get a glass oil remover spray or adding soap inwind shield water tank, keep a potato in your car. Cut it in half & rub it on your side mirror glass. This will not allow water droplets to accumulate on the mirror. You can try this on other glasses too.

- **Defensive Driving Key 5. Navigating Tough areas during rains:**
- Steer clear of flooded regions and water-logged zones while driving, whenever feasible.
- If driving through water is necessary, make sure the water is not too deep that will create risk for your car and life and if you feel safe enough -drive cautiously in low gear to prevent water from getting into the engine.
- *Mostly water enters though exhaust of your car, so maintain a steady acceleration that will help in generating back pressure at exhaust which will resist water entry inside.*

— If, for any reason, you are forced to get out of the car, keep an eye out for potential electrical short circuits and wear shoes or other anti-electric gear.

# Module 4

# Emergency Response Measures in Varying Road & Traffic Situations

The guidebook opens with an overview of the importance of road safety in India, including important data and the goals of the manual. It provides background information on why this guide is essential for all drivers driving on varying roads and traffic conditions in India. An outline of the current state of road safety in India is given in this section, together with information on typical causes of accidents and the laws that control them. It is essential to make sure your car is in good working order and that you are ready for anything before you get on the road. This section discusses personal safety equipment, car upkeep, and what should be in every emergency kit. Discover how to drive defensively, understand traffic signs and signals, obey speed limits, and handle different types of road conditions as well as unexpected situations. This extensive section describes the different kinds of road emergencies and how to respond to them. It offers detailed instructions on how to evaluate circumstances, guarantee safety, call emergency services, and give basic first aid. Knowing what to do in the unfortunate event of an accident can make a big difference. This section describes what needs to be done right away, There is a wide range of driving situations. This section discusses the difficulties of driving in inclement weather, at night, and when there are other vulnerable road users. It also goes over how to handle dangerous items safely. Important state and national emergency numbers are included in this fast reference section, along with phone numbers for law enforcement, medical services, and roadside help. The goal of this guidebook is to serve as a thorough reference that gives drivers in India the skills and information they need to drive safely and handle emergencies.

## 4.1 Handling Hydroplaning

- Hydroplaning is a phenomenon created when water makes a layer between the road and the tire
- If your car begins to hydroplane/float, do not brake abruptly or become panicked.
- Until you feel the road grip & regain control, ease off the accelerator and steer straight.

Fig. **What is Hydroplaning for a car**

## 4.2 Stalled Engine in Water

- If the engine stalls in the water, do not attempt to restart it. Serious engine damage may result from this.
- If the water level rises, get out of the car safely and go somewhere higher.

## 4.3 How to Avoid a Sudden Obstacle?

**Brake and Steer technique**: In case of an unexpected object that you wish to avoid, assess the space in the side lane, apply brake first, and then steer firmly into the obstacle's side space. Following this sequence will make your stable move while missing the obstacle.

## 4.4 Accident Response

– If you are in a minor accident, get to a safe place, get first aid done
– To warn other drivers, use caution triangles and hazard lights.
– Make a call to emergency services, being sure to include precise details about the occurrence and your location.

## 4.5 First Aid Basics: It Helps a Lot if You Know This

– Acquire the knowledge of basic first aid and CPR procedures to treat wounds and heart troubles of co-passengers until medical assistance comes.
– Maintain an accessible and up-to-date first-aid kit.

**ALL INDIA ON-ROAD EMERGENCY HELP NUMBERS**

| | Your Emergency Need<br>(Pl. refer for more local helpline numbers on boards displayed on Highways) | Dial |
|---|---|---|
| 1 | **Polic control Room** | **100** |
| 2 | **Women's Help Line** | **181** |
| 3 | **Medical Helpline** | **108** |
| 4 | **Ambulance Helpline** | **102** |
| 5 | **Fire Service** | **101** |

- **Basic self Help: Replacing a flat Tire on your car**
- Put a warning triangle, or if you don't have one, use anything safe that can attract the attention of other cars coming toward you (fig.no.1)
- Use wheel spanner to loosen and tighten wheel nuts ( fig.n.2)
- Use your car jack to lift the car as shown (fig. no.3 and 4)

(fig.no.1)

(fig.no.2)　　　　(fig.no.3)　　　　(fig.no.4)

# Special Considerations for Indian Roads

India's road network is remarkably diverse, encompassing both tranquil rural roads and busy urban motorways. This chapter gives drivers the knowledge and advice they need to drive these roads safely. Major thoroughfares with heavy traffic that link states and cities. State-maintained roads that connect various areas within a state. Smaller, frequently poorly maintained roadways that link rural and village regions. Roads are found in cities and towns that are known for having a lot of traffic and plenty of intersections. Usually found in rural and some urban highways, cautious navigation is required. Frequently deficient, with cars of all sizes carelessly sharing the road. It can be erratic, particularly in rural locations; always remain cautious. Make sure your car has a jack, an emergency tool kit, and a spare tire. Always be on the lookout for potential threats, such as animals, pedestrians, and abrupt stops. Keep your distance from other cars at a safe distance. Mirrors are frequently used to keep an eye on oncoming vehicles. Respect the posted speed limits, which might differ significantly based on the area and kind of road. In residential areas close to markets, particularly in school zones, exercise extra caution. Be ready to share the road with trucks, buses, and bicycles, among other types of vehicles. Be mindful of non-motorized road users, such as animals and pedestrians.

- Get yourself aware of the laws and ordinances governing traffic in your area.
- Drivers and passengers all over India are required to wear seat belts.

- In case of emergency, remain composed and, if you can, relocate to a secure area. Make a call to emergency services and give precise details.
- Understand the customs of the area; these can differ greatly from state to state. Every state in India has its own culture, language, and traditions.
- Be aware of things you carry in the car, especially liquor, as some states prohibit them.
- Language barriers might arise in rural locations; thus, it can be useful to know some simple words in the local tongue.
- You may guarantee a safer and more pleasurable driving experience by being aware of the peculiarities of Indian roads and according to the safety advice provided in this book.

To help create a safer driving environment for you and all road users, always be aware of your surroundings, be aware of driving behaviors of others around.

## 5.1 Awareness of Local Hazards

- Recognize the typical monsoon-related risks in the region you are visiting, including potholes, landslide zones, tunnels, under development, and bad road conditions.
- For up-to-date information, subscribe to local news and weather updates.

## 5.2 Dealing with the Traffic

- **Patience and Alertness** are 2 key aspects that will help no matter what you face on the way.
- Exercise caution and patience when in heavy traffic. Significant delays can occur due to monsoon rainfall.
- Take into account unexpected events with other road users, surprising guests (cows, etc) on the road, carts, pedestrians, or vehicle breakdowns. Try not to panic or become anxious; instead, wait and cooperate with others on the road in a way that helps clear the way for everyone.
- Observe traffic laws and signals, even when others don't. Driving defensively is essential.

## 5.3 Surprising Guests on the Indian Roads: People/ Animal Crossings

- **It is not unusual** if you find anyone or anything unexpected on Indian roads without a warning
- **Stay alert** for people walking, bicyclists, and animals who are crossing or looking for cover or need to cross the road, especially when it's raining. Please consider they are not under any shelter, you are. Stop…. take a step back -if needed and allow them to pass first.
- If needed, slow down and honk your horn gently to warn them.
- If you suspect other road users as a troublemaker for you, stay away, catch up a safe place, use emergency support contact number, but this happens in rare case.

## 5.4 Five-Key Traffic offenses and consequences (2024) in India:

| | Traffic Rule violated | Fine or legal action |
|---|---|---|
| 1 | Drunk driving or driving under influence of intoxicated items | • **Rs.10000/- and/or 6 month imprisonment or Rs.15000/- and 2 years imprisonment** |
| 2 | Over speeding above area/zone speed limits | • **Rs.5000/-** |
| 3 | Dangerous driving /Using the vehicle in hazardous conditions. | • **First Offense: Rs.1,000 to Rs.5,000, license seizure, and/or 6 months to 1 year in prison**<br>• **Second Offense: Rs.10,000, license seizure, and up to 2 years in prison** |
| 4 | Signal jumping | • **Rs.1,000 to Rs.5,000, license seizure, and/or 6 months to 1 year in prison** |
| 5 | Not driving in the proper lane | • **Court order** |

# Key Takeaway

In India, safe driving during the monsoon-like seasons, as well as varying traffic situations, necessitates a blend of vehicle readiness, defensive driving techniques, and contextual awareness. You may greatly lower your risk of driving in hazardous and wet circumstances by adhering to these suggestions and strategies. In India, driving safely necessitates being alert, organized, patient, and flexible to changing driving circumstances. Drivers can greatly increase their own safety and the safety of others by adhering to pre-driving procedures, using defensive driving strategies, being aware of emergency response protocols, and comprehending the particularities of Indian roadways. Always put safety first, be aware of the state of the road, and drive with composure under all circumstances.

- **5-Most Important Things to Remember While You Drive in India:**

  1. Prepare yourself, your legal documents, the information about your visiting area, and your car in advance.
  2. Be in the present, hyper-aware, and anticipate with tips given in this book.
  3. Take breaks every 1-2 hours in long drives. Stop at a safe place when you feel tired.
  4. Adhere to traffic rules & signals -even if you see others around who don't.
  5. Use the horn responsibly and effectively to avoid triggering irritation in others.

Source: NCRB2022, Transport Research Wing 2023

- **WHY SHOULD YOU FOLLOW THIS GUIDE?**

You are not just improving your driving and saving lives, but you are also transforming your life, contributing to environmental protection, economy and sustainability!

✓ **Tips for Environment Protection**
  - Always maintain your car properly, including tires, to reduce the rate of carbon footprint increase.
  - Use maximum eco-friendly products on journeys, and avoid the use of plastic.
  - Avoid rapid acceleration, heavy braking, and unnecessary honking, which can increase fuel consumption, emissions, and noise pollution.
  - Turn off your engine when you are idle for more than one minute in one place.
  - Consider Hybrid or Electric vehicles when you are buying a new car.

# A Complementary Life Transformation Tip

Try this with your driving:

- STOP HONKING at all for small reasons. Wait, think about the situation ahead of your car from different angles, from another person's perspective.
- Use your Horn Only, Only, and Only -when it is the utmost requirement for safety.
- Observe the change in the patience and calmness in your daily routines after a few weeks from the day you started this and made it a habit.
- Observe the change in your interactions with others and the results you are getting out of it. Compare it with your life before this habit. You are also contributing to reducing Noise pollution.

Thank you for being part of the "Drive to Thrive" movement!

Drive responsibly, Stay Safe…. Enjoy and learn about the incredible diversity of India!

www.ingramcontent.com/pod-product-compliance
Lightning Source LLC
Chambersburg PA
CBHW021148130726
47988CB00004B/1517